Bald Eagles

Surprise!

SCHOLASTIC

Library of Congress Cataloging-in-Publication Data
Title: Bald eagles
Description: New York, NY: Children's Press, an imprint of Scholastic Inc., 2020. | Series: Wild Life LOL! | Includes index.
Identifiers: LCCN 2019006035| ISBN 9780531240335 (library binding) | ISBN 9780531234860 (paperback)
Subjects: LCSH: Bald eagle—Juvenile literature.
Classification: LCC QL696.F32 B354 2020 | DDC 598.9/43—dc23

Produced by Spooky Cheetah Press

Design by Anna Tunick Tabachnik

Contributing Jokester: J. E. Bright

No part of this publication may be reproduced in whole or in part, or stored in a retrieval system, or transmitted in any form or by any means, electronic, mechanical, photocopying, recording, or otherwise, without written permission of the publisher. For information regarding permission, write to Scholastic Inc., Attention: Permissions Department, Scholastic Inc., 557 Broadway, New York, NY 10012.
© 2020 Scholastic Inc.

All rights reserved. Published in 2020 by Children's Press, an imprint of Scholastic Inc.

Printed in Heshan, China 62

SCHOLASTIC, CHILDREN'S PRESS, WILD LIFE LOL!™, and associated logos are trademarks and/or registered trademarks of Scholastic Inc.

1 2 3 4 5 6 7 8 9 10 R 29 28 27 26 25 24 23 22 21 20

Scholastic Inc., 557 Broadway, New York, NY 10012.

Photographs ©: cover, spine: Tom Walker/Getty Images; cover speech bubbles and throughout: pijama61/iStockphoto; cover speech bubbles and throughout: Astarina/Shutterstock; back cover: Charles Schug/iStockphoto; 1: Colin Edwards Wildside/Shutterstock; 2: Teri Virbickis/Shutterstock; 3 top: Josh Miller Photography/Getty Images; 3 bottom: Teri Virbickis/Shutterstock; 4: Fritz Polking/Minden Pictures; 5 child silo: Nowik Sylwia/Shutterstock; 5 eagle sitting: Gpgroup/Dreamstime; 5 eagle flying: Lnmstuff/Dreamstime; 6-7: Gary Vestal/Getty Images; 8-9: sianc/iStockphoto; 10 inset: VisionsbyAtlee/iStockphoto; 10-11: Lynn M. Stone/Minden Pictures; 12: KenCanning/iStockphoto; 13 left: Alan Murphy/Minden Pictures; 13 right: David Osberg/Getty Images; 14: Doug Allan/Minden Pictures; 15 top left: cturtletrax/iStockphoto; 15 top right: Visuals Unlimited,Inc./Joe McDonald/Getty Images; 15 bottom left: MikeLane45/iStockphoto; 15 bottom right: Jpiks1/Dreamstime; 16-17: Sylvain Cordier/Minden Pictures; 18: RC Reid Photography/Shutterstock; 19 left: Bruce Lichtenberger/Getty Images; 19 right: Paul Nicklen/Getty Images; 20: Natural Planet/Pete Ryan/Media Bakery; 21 left: bazilfoto/iStockphoto; 21 right: Danita Delimont/Getty Images; 21 bottom: predrag1/iStockphoto; 22: Arthur Morris/Getty Images; 23 left: Klaus Nigge/Getty Images; 23 right: Mark Newman/Minden Pictures; 24-25: James L. Amos/Getty Images; 25 bottom right: Tom & Pat Leeson/KimballStock; 26 left: Kobby Dagan/Dreamstime; 26 right: Dorothea Lange/Library of Congress; 27 left: USFWS Photo/Alamy Images; 27 right: Patrick Frischknecht/Robert Harding; 28 left: nicholas_dale/iStockphoto; 28 right: Neil_Burton/iStockphoto; 29 top: Sergey Uryadnikov/Shutterstock; 29 bottom: Alan Murphy/BIA/Minden Pictures; 30 top: Charles Schug/iStockphoto; 30 map: Jim McMahon/Mapman®; 30 bottom: Tetra Images/Superstock; 31: Design Pics Inc./Getty Images; 32: Jak Wonderly/Getty Images.

TABLE OF CONTENTS

Meet the Majestic Bald Eagle............... 4
A Bald Eagle's Body 6
Zooming In 8
A Home in the Sky 10
Gone Fishin' 12
Also on the Menu 14
Love Is in the Air 16
Home, Sweet Home 18
A Safe Place for Babies.................... 20
Spreading Their Wings..................... 22
Ancient Eagles 24
Bald Eagles and People.................... 26

Wow!

Bald Eagle Cousins 28
The Wild Life 30
Index 32
About This Book........... 32

MEET THE MAJESTIC BALD EAGLE

Are you ready to be amazed and amused? Keep reading! This book will send you soaring.

I really DO look majestic, don't I?

LOL!
What kind of animal doesn't need a comb?
A bald eagle!

At a Glance

Where do they live? → Bald eagles live only in North America, from Alaska and Canada to Mexico.

What do they do? → Eagles spend much of their time searching for something to eat!

What do they eat? → Bald eagles' diet can be varied, but their favorite food is fish.

What do they look like? → Bald eagles are large birds with bright yellow beaks and feet.

How big are they?

Hint: They're probably not as tall as you. Check this out:

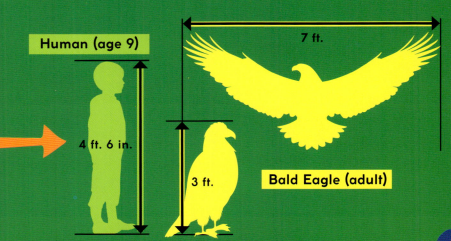

Human (age 9) — 4 ft. 6 in.

Bald Eagle (adult) — 7 ft., 3 ft.

A BALD EAGLE'S BODY

Bald eagles are **raptors**. They are built to hunt!

Look Sharp! An eagle's powerful feet have four toes with sharp claws, called talons.

THAT'S EXTREME! A bald eagle can fly carrying a fish that's half its own body weight.

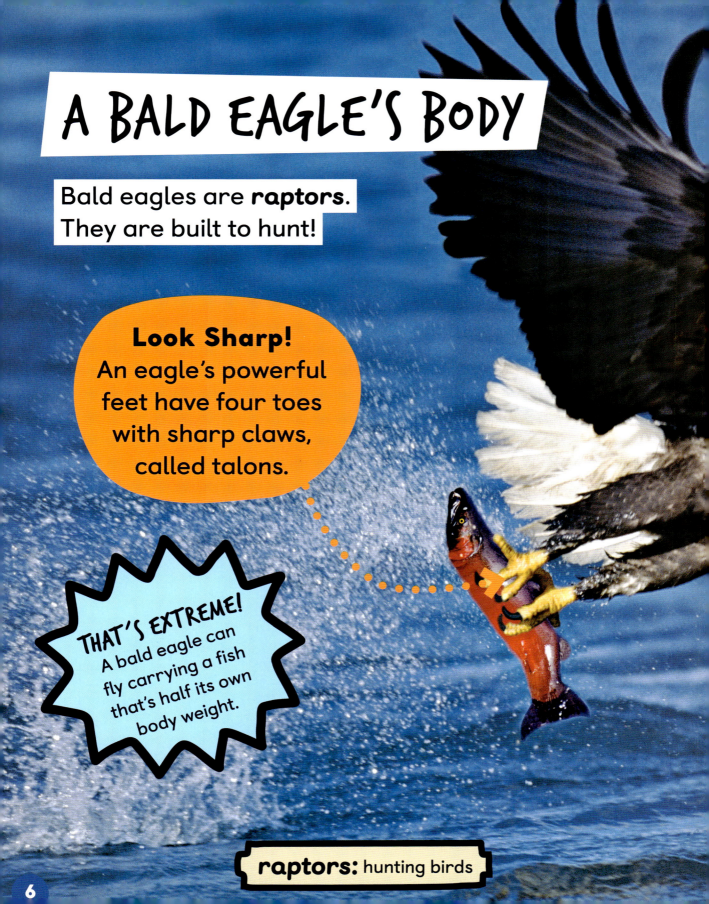

raptors: hunting birds

That's a Stretch! An eagle's wingspan can reach 7 feet. That is wider than an adult person is tall!

WACKY FACT: Bald eagles aren't really bald. Their heads are covered in white feathers.

Eagle Eyes Bald eagles can see four times as well as a person with perfect vision.

Gotcha!

Grip and Rip An eagle's beak has a hook at the tip for tearing into food.

ZOOMING IN

A bald eagle's most powerful weapon is its black talons. Check them out!

Slice and Dice
Sharp talons are used to slice into **prey**.

THAT'S EXTREME!
Male and female bald eagles look alike. But females are 25% larger.

WACKY FACT: An eagle's talons keep it from falling off a branch while it sleeps!

prey: an animal that is killed by another animal for food

A HOME IN THE SKY

Bald eagles can live almost anywhere. The greatest number are found in Alaska.

Without my warm feathers, I'd be a frozen BRRR-d.

WACKY FACT: Bald eagles are also known as sea eagles.

A Water View
Eagles' favorite places to live are near water and have lots of tall trees. That gives them a place to live—and to hunt.

Dinner Party
Bald eagles mostly live alone or in pairs. But they often gather in large groups to feed.

Fantastic Feathers

Bald eagles have no problem with Alaska's cold weather. They have 7,000 feathers that keep them warm.

At Home in the Skies

Eagles flap their wings to take off, but very often they **glide** through the sky to save energy.

THAT'S EXTREME! A soaring eagle can reach speeds of up to 45 miles per hour. That's speedier than the fastest racehorse can run.

glide: to fly without flapping the wings

GONE FISHIN'

Bald eagles really like to eat fish, such as salmon, herring, shad, and catfish. Here's how they catch them!

Let's see what I see in the sea.

THAT'S EXTREME! Fish make up at least half of a bald eagle's diet.

WACKY FACT: Bald eagles can paddle through the water to catch a fish.

1

Eye Spy . . .
A bald eagle can spot a fish from up to 1 mile away. The bird zooms out of the sky as it dives toward its prey.

LOL!
Why couldn't the fish see the eagle? Because it was in da skies (disguise).

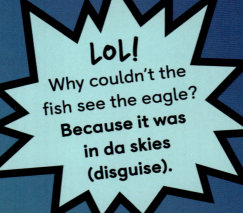

2

Gotcha!
When it is right over the fish, the eagle spreads its wings to slow down. Then it drives its talons into the fish and lifts it up in its claws.

3

I'll Take Mine to Go
If the fish isn't too heavy, the eagle will fly to its nest. If the fish is too heavy, the eagle carries its meal to shore and eats all it can.

ALSO ON THE MENU...

Although bald eagles prefer fresh fish, they are not picky eaters. They eat lots of other animals—and even rotting meat.

WACKY FACT: Bald eagles often steal food from other birds of prey.

I was eating that!

I am SOAR-y.

remains of a whale

snakes

turtles

Bald eagles enjoy these foods, too.

rabbits

puffins

15

LOVE IS IN THE AIR

When bald eagles reach four or five years old, they are ready to start a family. Before becoming a pair, the male and female see if they are a good fit.

LOL!
What did the eagle give her mate?
A peck on the cheek.

WACKY FACT: Bald eagle pairs stay together for life. That can be as long as 20 years.

1

Meeting Up

At first, the eagles fly together. They sit in the same tree together and look for fish in the water below.

2
Let's Talk
As they grow closer, the eagles call out to each other as they hunt.

3
Hang On Tight!
As a final test, the birds lock talons and spin through the air at top speed. Just before hitting the ground, they unhook and fly up again. They are ready to be a pair.

17

HOME, SWEET HOME

Once a male and a female become a pair, they begin to build their nest. They look for a high tree near a fishing spot.

THAT'S EXTREME! The biggest bald eagle nest ever found was 9½ feet around and 20 feet deep!

Pick-Up Sticks
The birds grab branches and carry them to the site.

WACKY FACT: If eagles reuse a nest, they will enlarge it by 1 or 2 feet every year.

This nest will be great if I just STICK with it!

Careful Crafting

The birds use their beaks and talons to weave the sticks together. They add moss and leaves to the inside.

A Cozy Home

This will be a safe place to lay eggs and raise baby eagles. The eagles may continue to use the nest year after year.

A SAFE PLACE FOR BABIES

The mother eagle usually lays two eggs, but she can lay as many as four. She and the father take turns **incubating** them.

Keeping Watch
The mother and father protect the eggs from owls and raccoons.

Craaaaack!
After about 35 days, the eggs are ready to hatch. They don't all hatch at once.

Firstborn
The first bird to hatch may kill its siblings so it doesn't have to share food!

incubating: keeping eggs warm before they hatch

SPREADING THEIR WINGS

Baby eagles are called chicks. They look very different from their parents!

Mom says I'm the cutest.

THAT'S EXTREME! Eagles grow by about 1 pound every four days. It takes about 8½ weeks for them to reach adult size.

1

Little Fuzz Balls

The chicks are covered in light feathers called down. They snuggle close to their parents to stay warm. The babies need a lot of food to grow.

WACKY FACT: It takes five years for a bald eagle's head feathers to turn white.

ANCIENT EAGLES

Scientists think the ancestor of birds was a birdlike dinosaur that lived 150 million years ago. Scientists discovered this by studying **fossils** like this one.

THAT'S EXTREME!
The oldest bald eagle fossil is 1 million years old!

What's Your Name?
This animal is called *Archaeopteryx*, which means "old wing."

Feathered Friend
This fossil clearly shows that *Archaeopteryx* had feathers.

fossils: plants or animals from millions of years ago preserved as rock

BALD EAGLES AND PEOPLE

We go back a long way!

Some Native Americans use eagle feathers in ceremonial clothing.

1700s

There were close to half a million bald eagles in North America. Many Native American tribes, or nations, thought of this beautiful and powerful bird as sacred.

1917 to 1952

In the state of Alaska, people were paid to kill bald eagles. It is believed that more than 100,000 eagles were shot for money during this period.

WACKY FACT: The bald eagle is the national bird of the United States.

This bald eagle is being cared for at an animal hospital.

1967

A pesticide called DDT was damaging bald eagle eggs, so fewer chicks were born. The birds were listed as an endangered species.

Free as a bird!

Today

After DDT was banned in the 1970s, bald eagles slowly began to recover. Today there are more than 70,000 bald eagles living in North America.

Bald Eagle Cousins

These are the bald eagle's closest cousins. They are all excellent fish hunters.

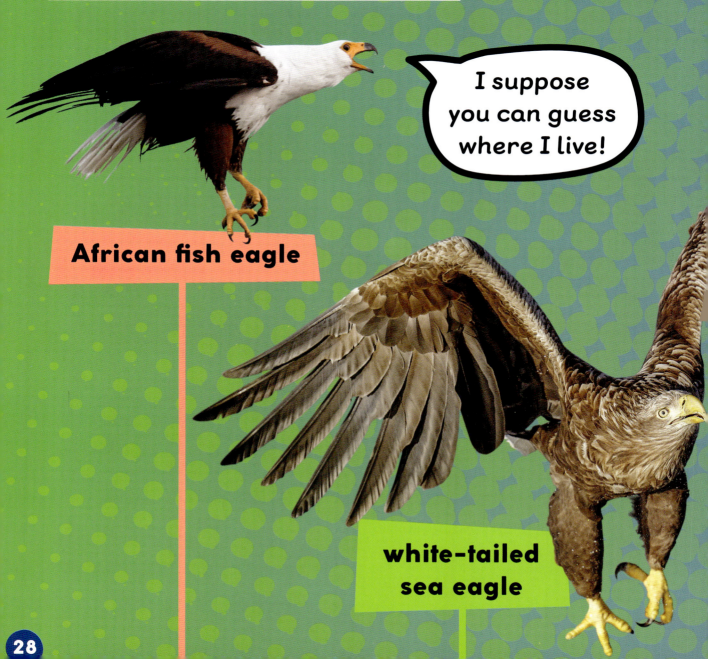

I suppose you can guess where I live!

African fish eagle

white-tailed sea eagle

The Wild Life

Look at this map of the world. The areas in red show where bald eagles live today: regions in North America. We want bald eagles to continue having **habitats** to live in. Otherwise, one day there might not be any red left on this map.

North America

habitats: the places where a plant or an animal makes its home

What Can You Do?

1 Bald eagles get most of their food from the water, so it's important that we keep Earth's oceans, lakes, rivers, and streams clean. **Don't litter!**

2 If you live in an area near a good fishing source, you might find bald eagle nests right in your neighborhood! Eagles make nests in lots of really high spots—not just trees. **If you see a nest, make sure you don't disturb it.**

3 **Speak up!** Tell everyone what you learned about bald eagles. The more people know about how important these birds are, the more people will want to protect them.

Yeah, BEAK up!

INDEX

Alaska 10, 11, 26	prey 8, 12–13, 14–15
Archaeopteryx 24–25	raptors 6
babies 19, 20, 22–23	starting a family 16–17
beak 7, 19	talons 6, 8–9, 13, 17, 19
body 6–7	trees 10, 16, 18
feathers 7, 11, 22, 24, 26	vision 7, 12
flying 11, 13, 16, 23	water 10, 12, 16
hunting 7, 10, 12–13, 17	wings 7, 11, 13, 23
nest 13, 18–19	

ABOUT THIS BOOK

This book is a laugh-out-loud early-grade adaptation of *Bald Eagles* by Dr. Hugh Roome. *Bald Eagles* was originally published by Scholastic as part of its Nature's Children series in 2019.

Now take it to the NEST level!